# FILOMENA, DAUGHTER OF LIGHT

A Yuruti Indian Woman Brings the Light of Christ
to Her People in the Amazon Jungle.

# FILOMENA, DAUGHTER OF LIGHT

A Yuruti Indian Woman Brings the Light of Christ
to Her People in the Amazon Jungle.

Filomena Acuña Romero

*Filomena: Daughter of Light* – Filomena Acuña Romero

Copyright © 2016

First edition published 2016

All rights reserved. No part of this book may be reproduced, stored in a retrieval system, or transmitted in any form or by any means – electronic, mechanical, photocopying, recording, or otherwise, without written permission from the publisher.

*Cover Design: BookCoverLabs.com*

*eBook and Audiobook Icons: Icon design/Shutterstock, Ganibal/Shutterstock*

*Editors: Donna Sundblad and Charlotte Graber*

Printed in the United States of America

Aneko Press – *Our Readers Matter*™

www.anekopress.com

Aneko Press, Life Sentence Publishing, and our logos are trademarks of

Life Sentence Publishing, Inc.
203 E. Birch Street
P.O. Box 652
Abbotsford, WI 54405

**BIOGRAPHY & AUTOBIOGRAPHY / Religious**

Paperback ISBN: 978-1-62245-283-5

eBook ISBN: 978-1-62245-284-2

10 9 8 7 6 5 4 3 2 1

Available where books are sold

# Contents

Introduction .................................................................................................... VII

**Part 1: My Early Visits to My People** ........................................................ 1

    Ch. 1: My First Trip to the Jungle ............................................................ 3

    Ch. 2: The River Trip and Visit to Puerto Loma ..................................... 9

    Ch. 3: A Yurutí Feast ................................................................................ 21

    Ch. 4: The First Rays of Light ................................................................. 33

    Ch. 5: My Parents Return to Puerto Loma ............................................ 39

**Part 2: Historical Interlude** ....................................................................... 41

    Ch. 6: My Father's Story ......................................................................... 43

    Ch. 7: The Rubber Trade ........................................................................ 47

    Ch. 8: Puerto Loma to Bonita Springs .................................................. 51

    Ch. 9: My Words Impact My Father ..................................................... 55

**Part 3: My Later Visits** ............................................................................... 57

    Ch. 10: My Father's Last Years ............................................................... 59

    Ch. 11: First Anniversary of My Father's Death ................................... 69

    Afterword ................................................................................................. 79

    Meet the Author ...................................................................................... 81

# Introduction

## by Patricia C. Stendal

I first met Filomena in 1982 in San Martin, Meta, a middle-sized town in eastern Colombia. She had come from her home in the far away southeastern jungles and was helping my daughter-in-law with the care of a new baby. Twenty-year-old Filomena desired to earn some money to help her physically handicapped youngest brother, so she accompanied a relative to San Martin where a position was secured with Marina, my oldest son Russell's wife. My first impression of Filomena was that she was a pleasant, serious-minded young woman, quite capable and willing to help with whatever task was at hand. Her Spanish was limited but adequate, and her Aunt Cecilia, Marina's mother, who had left the same tribe many years before, was able to orient her, using her own Yurutí language whenever necessary. The Yurutí are a small tribe, a branch of the larger Tucano tribe. Some eight small tribes compose the Tucano linguistic family. In addition to Spanish and the Yurutí language, Filomena was also conversant in most, if not all, of these other languages.

During the time Filomena lived with Marina, our son Russell was kidnapped by Marxist guerrillas. Russell's right-hand man, Guillermo (Bill) Romero, was supposed to have been shot and killed at the same time, but circumstances had prevented Bill from accompanying Russell in his small airplane that fateful day in August 1983. Many years before, our family had come from the United States to Colombia as missionaries to an Indian tribe in northern Colombia, but we were temporarily living in San Martin, the largest town in the eastern Colombian plains, to back up our adult sons who were establishing themselves as farmers, and in the case of Russell, as a jungle pilot in the region.

Since Russell was held captive far deeper in the jungle, Bill came to San Martin and before long announced that he and Filomena were getting married. Bill was from a respected family in Bogotá, and we were quite surprised that he wanted to marry an Indian woman; however Bill recognized the quality of character in Filomena, and after a lot of counseling by Aunt Cecilia, Bill and Filomena formed their own household.

While Russell was in captivity, his captors gave him a picture of himself and Bill. Bill was carrying a shotgun to be used as a survival weapon in case of an airplane crash over the jungle. To the subversives, it looked like Bill was the bodyguard. Their orders were to kidnap the pilot and kill the bodyguard. Upon his release, Russell was very surprised to find that Bill was in San Martin, married to Filomena. Russell showed Bill the picture and told him that his life was in danger. At the U.S. Embassy in Bogota, the officials were very happy that Russell was released safely and granted his request for visas for Bill and Filomena to travel to the USA with Russell and Marina and their baby daughter Lisa, who was now 16 months old.

In Bonita Springs, Florida, they all visited my husband's elderly parents. Bill hit it off very well with the grandparents. He had worked on cruise ships at one time, and in their younger years, the grandparents had enjoyed many cruises. Bill knew enough English to wait on them and recreate the atmosphere of the cruises that they had loved in the past. They invited Bill and Filomena to stay with them and care for them in their old age.

After many years, their tourist visas were expiring. The Romero's applied for permanent visas, green cards. When it looked like the visas might be denied, the neighbors, several pastors, and a number of churches joined forces to submit a petition that Bill and Filomena be allowed to stay. They saw how necessary the Colombian couple had become to the well-being of the elderly Americans. The visas were granted. But another problem arose. Bill and Filomena did not have the money to pay the fee of $35 each for their visas. Also, Grandpa had become very reluctant to purchase rice and other Colombian food the Romero's were used to eating. As Bill tells the story, "The refrigerator was bare."

Bill and Filomena had become serious Christians, and Bill felt he heard the Lord's voice in his heart saying, "Go to the store and buy $30 worth of the groceries that you need." They went to the local supermarket and obediently put $29 worth of food into their cart and headed for the check-out counter without a cent in their pockets. The register rang up $29.35.

At that moment, the man in line behind them spoke up, "I am paying for their food," he told the cashier, and to Bill he said, "Meet me outside."

Out in the parking lot, the stranger handed Bill $70 in cash. "I was told to give you $100," he said, "so here is the other $70." With that, the man climbed into his vehicle, and drive away. It was the last the Romero's saw of him. Bill believes he was an angel. Now they not only had food, but they also had the money to go ahead with their visas.

After a number of years, Filomena became very homesick for her family so far away in Colombia. Without a telephone number, Bill decided to try to call Mitú, the market town for the Yurutí, to see if he could get news of Filomena's family. First he dialed an operator in Bogotá, Colombia's capital city. When he told her he wanted to call Mitú, she connected him to an operator in Villavicencio, the gateway to the eastern plains and jungle. That operator connected him with an operator in Mitú. He told that operator about a little store on the edge of town where the Yurutí often came to buy their few provisions. The operator knew the store and connected him to the telephone there. To his great surprise, Filomena's sister, Margarita Acuña, answered the phone. She had just started working there the day before the call was made. After a few minutes of conversation with Filomena, the call was dropped, but the Yurutí, woman so far from home, was assured that her family was all right and that it was possible to call Mitú even without a telephone number.

By this time, Filomena knew quite a bit of English, and with his cruise ship experience, Bill found employment as a waiter in a high-end hotel. They saved money, and when the grandparents passed on, they used their savings as a down payment on a house of their own. A baby daughter was born, and in time Filomena found employment sewing draperies. They settled down in their own comfortable home and started to live the American dream.

It is against this backdrop that Filomena told me the following story.

# Part I

# My Early Visits to My People

### By Filomena Acuña Romero

# Chapter One

# My First Trip to the Jungle

With a heavy heart, I hung up the phone. The short call had come from far away. My brother Luis had spent some of his scarce money to let me know that our sister Margarita was living in desperate conditions. She was struggling to raise six children in dire poverty. Like me, she had married a Spanish-speaking man from outside of our tribe. Her husband worked as a farm laborer in the foothills of the Andes Mountains outside the city of Villavicencio, the capital of the state of Meta in eastern Colombia. Although Margarita worked on the farm too, their earnings were not enough to feed their large family. They sought shelter wherever they could find it, living for some time in an abandoned chicken coop.

As I settled into an easy chair and looked around at my comfortable home in southwest Florida, I mentally contrasted it with the word picture Luis had just painted in my mind of Margarita's living conditions. Across the living room, my beautiful fourteen-year-old daughter Ana Lucia played a video game. Even the puppy nestled in her lap was well-fed and thriving. A desire was born in my heart to help Margarita.

About six years earlier, I had received another phone call from Luis. He called to tell me that he was in the hospital, gravely ill and not expected to live. Since leaving my home deep in the jungle, I had come to know Jesus Christ as my Lord and Savior. I shared my testimony with Luis and urged him to commit his life to Christ. Following my instructions, Luis was not only born again but soon was healed as well. Now he attended a Bible school for Indians in Villavicencio, preparing to preach the gospel.

Louis also told me that along with Margarita, my parents, and other relatives deep in the jungle were suffering privation. Their clothing was wearing out, and they had no money to buy new garments.

Before the arrival of outsiders into their jungle home, they had dressed only in scanty clothing made from tree bark. Now they were embarrassed for outsiders to see them that way, so each person took their last garments, placed them in a plastic bag, and buried it in the ground. If outsiders arrived, they would retrieve their bag and be suitably clothed to receive the visitors. In the meantime, they wore the old-time garments of bark.

Knowing that all of my family was in great need, I began to collect used clothing and save money from my earnings. A few close friends helped me and soon I had several duffel bags of clothing and money to pay for my airplane ticket. Leaving my husband Bill and Ana Lucia in Florida, I boarded a plane for Bogotá, Colombia and then on to Villavicencio. It was July 2001.

I was so happy to meet Luis at the airport in Villavicencio, and the two of us started out to walk to the place where Margarita and her family were living. It was a two and a half hour walk, climbing the hills around the city. On the way, Luis told me about the Bible school. It had been started by Swiss missionaries to train Christian leadership for the Indian tribes of Colombia. The only requirement was that the students somehow find money to pay their transportation costs to the Bible school. Once there, all tuition and living expenses were free. The Indians would study for several months and then return to their homes to put into practice what they learned. Then hopefully, they would return the next year for another semester. Practical skills were also taught. Many of the Indian men learned carpentry and block laying as well as other construction skills. The women were taught how to

**Luis and me on our way to visit Margarita**

sew and cook and to raise their children in a healthy manner. Both Luis and his wife Patricia were just finishing their first semester.

As we neared the farm, Luis and I were greeted by Margarita's six children – Olga, Ricardo, Jose, Jorge, Carlos, and Nelsy. The oldest and youngest were girls with four brothers in the middle. Their ages ranged from 5 to 12. Margarita was very surprised to see me but set about to welcome us into her humble home. She and her two daughters prepared a meager meal, and after they ate, the children

**Margarita's children**

**Me and Margarita in her house**

**Margarita and her daughters preparing the meal**

**TV Time**

**Devotions with Uncle Luis**

settled down to watch TV on their little red television set, their one contact with the modern world. At bedtime, Luis, their preacher-to-be uncle, opened the Bible and shared a devotional with the family. Early the next morning without breakfast, the six children started out for their daily two-hour walk to school. Finding enough food to eat is always a big struggle for this family. Sometimes the children are able to get breakfast and lunch at school, and that is a big help. On other days, they have to go without.

I gave some of the clothing I had brought to Margarita for her family, and after three days, Luis and I headed back to Villavicencio for the next part of our trip, this time to my home deep in the jungles of

**Leaving the farm**

the Vaupés, another state of Colombia where my parents and the rest of the family lived. Margarita went with us to the city. Knowing that I was not used to so much walking, we stopped first at the farm where Margarita worked, and she borrowed a mule for me to ride. It was apparent that my visit had brought much joy to Margarita and her family.

**Margarita borrowed a mule for me**

Chapter Two

# The River Trip and Visit to Puerto Loma

Luis and I returned to the airport at Villavicencio and boarded an airplane to the remote jungle city of Mitú (pronounced "me too"), the capital of a state called the Vaupés. There, Luis helped me rent a large, twenty-passenger canoe with a motor, driver, and a crew.

**Trip on the Vaupes River**

One of our many sisters, Maria, who lives in Mitú with her family, accompanied us on the trip to our home village. Patricia, Luis' wife, and their two young daughters also joined us in the canoe. We traveled downstream on the vast Vaupés River, until we reached Caño Yi, which is a tributary stream. Here we entered the *caño* and traveled upstream. When we came to swift rapids flowing over rocks, all of us passengers had to get out and walk alongside the large canoe, while the crew maneuvered it through the white water by pulling it from the shore. At the head of the rapids, we all climbed back into the canoe and continued upstream.

**Starting the Portage**

Finally, we arrived at a small village where our half-brother Moses and his family lived. From here, we walked for two hours on a small trail through the jungle to the Caño Paca where our family lived. The whole trip, from Mitú to my home village of Puerto Loma, took three days.

**My half-brother Moises and his family**

**On the trail**

Our family was surprised and very happy to see us, especially me. My mother and sisters had just prepared a fish soup and invited me to sit down and eat with them. Meanwhile, the children ran through the village, telling family members in the area about our arrival. People started to gather to welcome me, and soon twenty-five people had assembled. They were delighted to receive the clothing I had brought from home. To make sure each person received at least one garment, I had to break up cute little outfits. I gave the shirt or blouse to one child, and the pants or skirt to another. Soon, I had distributed all the clothing, except for a few special dresses I brought for my mother. Patricia also distributed some skirts she made at Bible school. My relatives immediately put on their new clothes. Our brother Alberto tried on one of the skirts for fun and everyone laughed. We all agreed the skirt looked better on his wife, Cecilia.

**My happy homecoming**

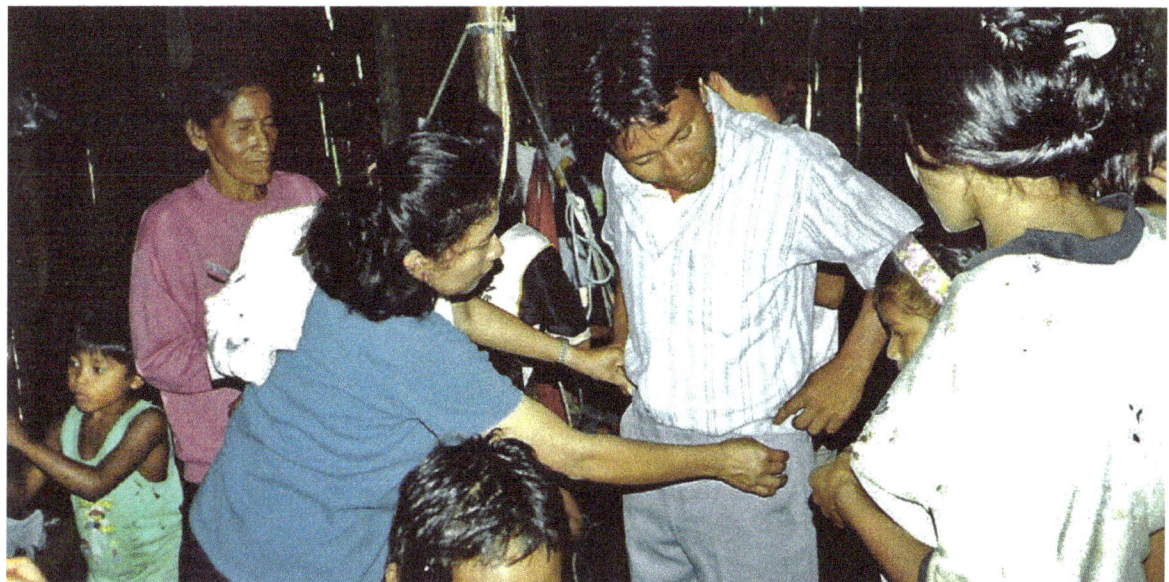
Trying on my gifts

Patricia made skirts at Bible School. My brother tried one on

**Luis passes out Bibles**

**Alberto and Carlos receive Bibles and tracts**

Some of the adults had attended school in Mitú and learned to read Spanish. They taught the younger ones to read as well. Luis had brought Bibles, New Testaments, and tracts from the Bible school, all in Spanish. After Patricia and I finished handing out the clothing, Luis distributed the Bibles. They were well received. Even my old father (the man with the bare chest in the picture) showed excitement about the Bibles. A husband and wife team from the Wycliffe Bible Translators had started to study our language with the goal of giving us a New Testament in our own language, but for now, the people were happy to have the Spanish literature, even if they didn't understand it very well.

**Everyone is happy with their Bibles**

At mealtime, in my village, the people sit on a long bench on one side of the house. Usually the women eat together and the men eat together. For some reason, Luis sat on the ground by the kettles. Everyone laughed until he found a seat on the bench beside our brother Alberto.

**The men at meal time**

**The women at meal time**

**Luis sitting on the floor**

**Luis found a place on a bench**

**Preparing the land for the new chapel**

After we ate, Luis proudly showed me the plot where the villagers had decided to build a small chapel. The next day work began, and every day while I was there, some of the people worked on preparing the ground and building the chapel.

**The next day the building started**

My mother and sisters tried to take good care of me as best they knew how; however, I missed my comfortable bed in Florida. I longed for a cup of coffee or hot chocolate and some rice to eat, or at least something different from the bread made from grated yuca and soup made from fish. All they had to drink was river water. Of course, most of all, I missed Bill and Ana Lucia. To me, the time went very slowly, but for my family in Colombia, my visit was over all too soon.

As the time drew near for me to return to Mitú, the first part of my homeward journey, the Yurutí people decided to give me a going-away party. According to tribal custom, this party is celebrated with flutes, traditional dances, and homemade liquor. I declined the liquor, as I didn't want to get intoxicated.

**Dance demonstration**

The time had been good, but I was ready to go home. The return trip was more difficult. This time, we traveled in a small canoe with no motor or crew. We all had to paddle, including me. My relatives didn't realize that after being away from the jungle for almost twenty years, my muscles were not strong and not used to paddling. However, I did the best I could. It wasn't so bad going downstream on Caño Yi, but when we came to the big Vaupés River, the going grew very hard as we struggled upstream against the current.

We finally arrived at Mitú, where Luis accompanied me to the airport. There, I said good-bye to my dear brother and boarded a flight to Villavicencio, changed planes there, and continued on to Bogotá. Upon arrival back in Miami, Bill and Ana Lucia met me, and we all cried with joy to see one another again. Together, we drove back to our cozy home in Bonita Springs, Florida. I felt safe and happy to be back, but in my heart, I was glad I had been able to do a little bit for my family deep in the jungle.

Back in Puerto Loma, the people were all happy. They started to pray and read the Bible.

**My last day with my family**

**They say goodbye**

# Chapter Three

# A Yurutí Feast

Back in my home in Florida, my thoughts were on my family in Colombia. I longed for a way to really help them. I wished someone would take an interest in them. They seemed so far away, and the trip to visit them was so costly and difficult. One of my main concerns was for Margarita and her husband and six children living in such poverty. I started to save money to help Margarita get a house.

By June 2002, I saved enough money to make another trip to Colombia. First, I landed in Bogotá and asked my friends there to help me open a bank account to start saving money for a house for Margarita. I hoped she would be able to buy a lot and build a house. It was the best I could do. I was able to get that set up before I took an airplane flight to Villavicencio

**My second trip to visit Margarita**

for a short visit with Margarita. Her husband, Ismael, was there this time. He seemed to be an agreeable man, doing the best he could to support his family.

They were happy so see me

I met Margarita's husband Ismael

Margarita and I with her daughters

Ismael and his sons

**Mitu before it was bombed**

From Villavicencio, I took a flight to Mitú, where Luis arranged for a canoe and motor for our trip to Caño Paca where our family lives. Once again, we traveled downstream on the huge Vaupés River in the dugout canoe. At Caño Yi, we turned upstream to pass through the five or more rapids. Some took

**Trip on the river**

a half hour or more to navigate. Finally, we arrived at the headwaters of Caño Yi where we found a tall fallen tree blocked our progress. After some time, we maneuvered the canoe under the tree and continued until the Caño grew so shallow we could go no farther. We had to take the trail that led to Caño Paca.

**Trip on the river**

Three days after leaving Mitú, we arrived at our jungle home. I was so happy to see my mother and father. They were old, and their health was not good. Worry always lingered at the back of my mind that they might pass away before I could see them again. They proudly showed me the roof erected for their new chapel.

**The chapel now has a roof**

Luis and Patricia were returning from four months at Bible school. Luis found that the thatched roof on his house had been damaged in his absence, so immediate repairs were necessary.

Everyone was so happy to see me again, they wanted to do something special for me. The men started working on special handcrafts to give me. My brother-in-law Francisco worked on a yuca squeezer, and others made items from jungle materials, mostly wild cane. The women worked on baskets and brooms. Then they decided to make a big special meal, a feast.

**Men and women making gifts**

The women brought yuca and firewood from their gardens. Alberto went hunting and brought back a wild turkey and an animal called a *guartinaja*. Alberto also brought boards to make benches, as Luis planned to invite our neighbors from a nearby village to the feast. These people were also a part of the Yurutí tribe, but were not quite so closely related to us as those who lived in Puerto Loma. They are cousins, but a little more distant.

**Women bringing food and firewood**

**Alberto with the guatanaje**

**Marta with the wild turkey**

**Alberto brings boards for benches**

The next day, the women started to prepare the yuca. Although there is another kind of yuca grown in other parts of Colombia called sweet yuca (it is not sweet but more like a potato and requires no special treatment), the yuca which grows in our thin jungle soil is called bitter yuca, or manioc. It contains a poisonous juice that must be extracted before it can be eaten.

**Peeling yuca**

Yuca is a root vegetable and grows something like a potato. The tubers must be harvested just before use since, unlike potatoes, the yuca rots once it is out of the ground. After harvesting, the yuca tubers are peeled and washed. Then they are grated. After grating, the mixture is washed again and stirred.

**Baby in homemade swing**

**Children help to strain the yuca**

After the yuca has been washed again, they put it into a round, loosely woven, basket-like container so the liquid can drain and carry the poisonous juices with it. Next, the mass is placed into a yuca squeezer, a long, thin tube woven out of wild cane. Each end of the yuca squeezer has a loop. One loop is attached to a pole or something a little bit high. A woman takes the other end and applies pressure at her end of the squeezer, using her body weight. The yuca squeezer is cleverly woven to contract and apply an immense amount pressure on the mass of grated yuca inside, extracting every last drop of poisonous liquid. This might sound risky, but it is just a normal procedure to the Yurutí. They don't even think about the bad results that could occur if all the poison isn't removed.

**Maria straining the washed yuca**

**Squeezing the yuca**

Once the poison is removed, they form the yuca mass into a very large, round, flat cake, like a huge tortilla or pancake. They bake it over a hot fire on a big, flat pan, made by them from a special kind of clay.

This is a lot of work. I tried to help, but was out of practice. I had been away from home too long to be able to do as well as my sisters. Our old mother helped too, but sometimes she just sat in a hammock and watched the babies. They even had a hand-made swing for the babies.

The Yurutí are not the only people to go through all this work to eat the bitter yuca. It is the staple of all the Indians and non-Indians living in the jungles of the Amazon basin, and they prepare it the same way. This large, round bread is called *casabe*.

The squeezed yuca pulp can also be toasted and stirred over a fire without making it into a round bread or cake. Prepared in this manner, it is called *fariña*. Fariña is something like what we eat in the United States called granola; however, it doesn't contain honey or sugar, or anything to give it a good taste. To those not used to it, the taste is rather bitter. Fariña is usually eaten with soup or some kind of liquid. I have been told the communist guerrillas carry enough fariña in their backpacks to keep them alive for thirty days, even if they can't find anything else to eat. Here in North America, our tapioca comes from the bitter yuca root.

**Making Fariña**

The liquid from the manioc is poisonous, but by boiling it, the poison is nullified. Sometimes the poisonous liquid is used to kill fish in the river. These two items, the bitter yuca and fish, are staples of the Yurutí diet. Sometimes they have fruit, avocados, and meat, but game is getting scarce in the area. And the Yurutí are not alone in this. The yuca plant is actually a staple in the jungle areas all over South America and Africa.

Finally the feast was ready. We all bathed in the river and dressed in our best clothes. Many wore clothing I had brought. Our guests arrived, and we all enjoyed an ample meal of fish soup, wild turkey soup, and guartinaja soup, along with casaba, farina, and *chicha* (a fermented beverage derived from maize). After the meal, Luis gave a little talk, welcoming me and bringing a short Christian message. Everyone had a good time and started to leave for their homes.

**The Feast**

Two days before I left to return home, they gave a presentation. They thought it funny to paint their legs as they used to do in the olden days before a fiesta. They only did this so I could take pictures of them. The men marched in a circle playing their flutes and carrying items they made as gifts. My elderly father thought this was very good. He wasn't used to wearing a shirt, and liked having his chest bare like in the olden days. At the end of the song, they placed all the gifts in a large basket and presented them to me to take home to the United States.

Men dancing

Painting Luis

Playing flutes

Presenting the gifts

## Chapter Four

## The First Rays of Light

At the end of 2003 money was scarce, so I wasn't able to take a trip to the Vaupés. In June 2004, Luis called me again. He said he was on his way to Bogotá and wanted to meet me there. I took two weeks off work and bought a ticket to Bogotá. Initially, I planned to only go as far as Bogotá to talk with Luis, but God had other plans.

When I arrived in Bogotá, I called Luis at the Bible Institute and received some shocking news. Luis could not travel to Bogotá. Alberto, our older brother who was the head man of the village of Puerto Loma, was so sick Luis had been named as his replacement. Our mother was also sick. Friends had bought Luis a ticket from Mitú to Bogotá. They decided I should use that ticket and reservation to go from Bogotá to Mitú. We agreed I could repay the friends later.

I flew to Mitú, where Luis and Margarita were waiting for me. I had wired money ahead for the canoe, motor, and supplies, and all was ready for the trip to Puerto Loma where our sick loved ones were. After the long river trip and the hike, we received a warm welcome from our family in Puerto Loma. Alberto and our mother were better. They claimed my coming was the best medicine they could have had. Soon they were up on their feet and walking around. I distributed the clothing, booklets, vitamins, and other gifts I had brought.

That first evening, we all gathered in the finished chapel for a devotional time. Luis led us in reading a Scripture passage and explaining it, and then we all prayed. I couldn't help but notice my old father had grown feebler, and now walked with the help of a big stick.

On this trip, my family decided to have a special Christian service in my honor, instead of the traditional feast they had held on my last visit two years before. They organized an early-morning prayer time in preparation for the special service. Luis and I expected few to attend this prayer time at six a.m., but to our surprise, everyone in the village came.

What a very special morning! The Holy Spirit moved upon the little group gathered in His name. Luis explained the passage on the fruit of the Spirit, especially the love of God manifested in the Christian towards others. He asked me how I could express the love of God towards the others. I said, "I think we can all be brothers and sisters, even those who are not blood relatives." Impressed by the Holy Spirit, I got up, went over to Alberto, and gave him a big hug. (Hugging and forms of expressing love are not common among the Yurutí.) Then I hugged Alberto's sixteen-year-old son, Carlos. My hug made a big impact on this young man. (The guerrillas were recruiting Carlos against his will.) Then I turned my attention to my cousin Hector. I felt the Lord wanted me to give him a big hug too, and tell him, "You are very special to God. The Lord is going to bless you and use you as His servant in this area." I admonished him to be alert to what God was going to do in his life.

Others giggled nervously, embarrassed by this intimate action. Soon they were silenced by the Holy Spirit, and became aware of something very

**Yurutí congregation**

important happening in the spiritual realm. I passed from one to the other, giving each one a hug and special words from God according to their need. Their hearts were touched, and unaccustomed tears sprang to their eyes.

At nine a.m., we realized we hadn't eaten yet. We all gathered in Luis' house to have breakfast, but a strange, ugly pressure in my chest led me to ask Luis to pray. We both knew the evil spirits of that place were not happy with what had happened. Luis and his wife Patricia prayed for me. My spirit was strengthened, but physically, my body was weak. To keep from fainting, I had to go lie down in a hammock and cover myself from head to toe with a blanket. I prayed, cried, and shook. My condition frightened my mother. "I'm all right," I assured her.

Luis also told everyone I would be okay. After I had prayed and wept for a while, Patricia brought me a very special breakfast and encouraged me to eat. After that, I was fine.

Everyone went off to do the work of the day. About four p.m., all was ready for the special meeting. Luis preached, and we all sang songs of praise led by my cousin Hector. Luis talked about spending time with the Lord, making good use of our time. Luis always opened the meeting up for comments and questions. Hector brought a teaching in the Yurutí language, explaining how Jesus had died and brought in a new covenant. He stressed that all the previous religious customs and contracts were now broken by Jesus' death and resurrection. I was touched to the heart to hear my cousin give this profound teaching in our native language. I too brought a short teaching in our Yurutí language.

Then we had supper of *cajuchi* (wild pig) and casaba. After eating, we all sang Christian choruses and played a tape of praise and worship which I had brought. I showed them how to dance in worship to the Lord. Everyone formed a circle, waved their hands in praise to the Lord, and jumped around, each one with their own unique step. After that, they sang songs of welcome to me, and then changed the words to make one of the songs into a good-bye song. This was all done instead of their usual tribal dancing to Colombian dance music that they were used to. After it was all over, I realized I had been so caught up in the praise and worship that I had forgotten to take pictures.

Their usual handcrafted gifts were completed the morning of my departure. It was time for me to pack up and leave. Many family members accompanied me to catch my flight in Mitú. Even my mother went along. She was so encouraged by all that had happened that she put aside her tremendous fear of the river, guerrillas, police, and army personnel.

My flight was scheduled to leave Mitú at eight a.m., but at seven a.m., we were stopped by an army patrol. They searched us and asked if we had seen the guerrillas. We were so many people traveling together the soldiers thought we must know something about the whereabouts of the subversives. We didn't know it at the time, but at that moment the guerrillas were on the other side of the river preparing an attack on the army. While we were being questioned, I heard my flight take off. The soldiers finally released our canoe. Half an hour later, the guerrillas attacked the army patrol at the same spot where our party had been delayed. In the ensuing battle, the lieutenant was killed.

Since my flight had left, we went four hours further downriver to the home of another of our family members, to wait three days for the next flight. The sound of fighting echoed in and around Mitú. On the day of the flight, we left at three a.m., paddling a small canoe in the dark to get to my flight. The water was swift and high; animal noises filtered from the jungle on both sides; and I knew guerrillas were all around. It all scared me to death. Luis started whistling Christian songs, but our mother hushed him for fear the guerrillas would come.

We arrived at Mitú safely at six a.m. We just had time to eat a hurried breakfast from the food we brought with us, and then rushed to the airport with all my baggage filled with the handcrafted gifts made for me. Once I checked in, the airport personnel wouldn't let me leave the airport, not even to go back to the house to say good-bye to my mother. The news filled me with sadness, knowing how disappointed my mother would be.

**My mother at the airport**

Luis jumped on a motorcycle and took off. Soon the roar of the motorcycle returned as Luis pulled up with our elderly mother riding on the back. Somehow she mustered the courage, not only to brave the raging river and the armed insurgents, but even to undertake a two or three mile ride on the back of a motorcycle to see me off on my way back to the United States.

While my mother braved the trip to see me off, she had another reason to visit Mitú. She hoped to consult a doctor there. But the money I had brought was gone, and after the death of the army officer, many soldiers flooded into the area. She didn't see the doctor, and the Yurutí returned to Puerto Loma again.

After this trip, once in a while, Luis called from Mitú. Our family members all came to faith in the Lord and supported Luis in his ministry. However, people in the surrounding villages were not all happy with the new message. Luis had visited those villages and brought them the gospel. He invited them all to the little chapel at Puerto Loma.

Luis felt it important to spend time in Puerto Loma to teach those who wanted to follow the Lord, but his two daughters also needed to be in Mitú to go to school. He spent as much time as possible in Puerto Loma, where he stressed reconciliation between brothers and family members and forgiveness of long-time grudges and hurts. Little by little, a handful of people from the other villages started visiting the little chapel. The Lord worked in the hearts of some who were very much against Luis and his message. As they watched the lives of Luis and his family, they were convinced Christianity really did make a difference.

Luis continued to reach out beyond his own village. He liked to make special meals and plan events just to invite the surrounding people to visit Puerto Loma to hear the gospel. His biggest problem was the ever-present lack of money.

## Chapter Five

## My Parents Return to Puerto Loma

In early 2005, Luis and Patricia, along with two other Yurutí couples, made their way by canoe to Mitú, hoping to fly to Villavicencio for another semester at the Bible Institute. To their disappointment, the expected money for their airplane tickets had not arrived. Sadly, they set out on the three-day canoe trip back to Puerto Loma.

Later in the year, I received a call from Luis. Both of our elderly parents were sick, and Margarita had agreed to take care of them in Villavicencio. He asked me to meet them in Villavicencio. I bought an airline ticket and met them there on the agreed date. Although my mother's lungs had been damaged by so many years of cooking over a smoky fire, my father was in a worse condition and hospitalized.

With the money I sent for Margarita, she had managed to acquire a small house by the side of the trail on the way up to the remote farm where she worked. It was a much better place to raise her family. She had installed a toilet and a place to wash clothes by hand, called a *lavadero*. She took our parents to this little house, after our father was released from the hospital. It wasn't easy to get them back and forth from the hospital in Villavicencio to the house due to their age, so she hired a vehicle.

My father was not happy with anything in Villavicencio or in Margarita's little house. It was too much of a change for him, and he made it clear he wasn't content. Margarita and I talked with the doctor in Villavicencio who attended him. The doctor advised us to take him back to his home in Puerto Loma. In spite of his advanced age and illnesses, the doctor believed he would live longer and be happier in Puerto Loma surrounded by his many children and grandchildren and the way of life familiar to him. I had mixed emotions as I bought tickets and arranged with Luis to secure a canoe to take them back to their home.

# Part II

# Historical Interlude

## Chapter Six

## My Father's Story

My father's name was Luis Acuña Valencia. His mother died when he was very young. He was the youngest child in the family; and, when he was about seven, his father realized he himself would not live much longer. He took my father to Mitú, a town in the jungle area, and asked some friends from the Spanish-speaking culture to take his boy and raise him. They agreed to take him, but his father made one strong request: They were not to send young Luis to school. His father wanted him to grow up in the same manner in which he had been raised and did not want him to be educated. The family honored my grandfather's request and did not enroll my father in school. They kept him at home, where he learned other skills. Being very bright, Luis learned how to count and handle money; however, he never did learn to read.

Mitú, the capital of the remote, southeastern department of Colombia called Vaupés, was an inland city which could only be reached by air. It had been established as a center for the rubber trade. From the Mitú airfield, the crude rubber was flown out to markets wherever rubber was needed. Cruel men, mostly from Brazil, controlled the harvesting of the rubber, and were very hard on the Indians who worked under them, tapping the rubber trees for their sap and making it into rolls of latex.

My father grew up in this atmosphere in Mitú where rubber was the dominant commodity. When he reached the age of eighteen or twenty years old, he decided to go back to the tribal area. With the flourishing rubber trade, he wanted to be a rubber boss. Only he determined to treat the Indians who worked under him fairly and with compassion, as he too was of Indian blood. He took out a loan from a bank and homesteaded a virgin area on the side of a mountain by the Vaupés River. With money from the bank, he bought a supply of trade goods – clothing, hammocks, salt, machetes, fishing gear, cooking pots, etc. – and went up and down the river, distributing his goods to Indians and asking them to come to his land to work for him. Although they took his goods, no one came to help him work. His land was between Caño Ti and Sircacia on the south side of the Vaupés River in a place he called Puerto Cerro, because it was high up and from that spot you could see a long ways up and down the river. This was his land to work in rubber gathering.

The Yurutí are one of the small tribes of the Tucano family. The custom is that a man has to marry a woman from a different related tribe. My father, having been raised in Mitú, didn't know anything about how to live out in the jungle on the land. A good thing happened to change that. He found his wife, a woman from the Curipaco tribe. In contrast to him, she knew how to do everything. The Curipacos differed slightly from the tribes of the Tucano family, but she taught him everything about working on his land. They were together for five years before she died. During their time together, they had three children. Two of them died young, but one girl, Emilia, survived. Upon her mother's death, Luis took Emilia to Mitú and left her in a boarding school there.

After spending five years alone, my father met my mother. My mother's name is also Emilia, the same as his oldest daughter. My mother came from the Cubeo tribe, one related to the Yurutí. Men from another village came to the Cubeo village where Emilia lived, and captured her along with other women to take to their home village to be their wives. Somehow, Emilia escaped from her captors. As my father, Luis, came down the caño in a canoe, he saw Emilia standing by a dock on the caño in an Indian community. She looked to him like a very good girl. He asked her to be his wife, and she said, "Yes."

I was the first child born to Luis and Emilia. My parents found a woman to take care of me so my mother could work on the farm. The babysitter's name was Elsa. However, Elsa was not a good babysitter. She fell in love with my father and followed him all around wherever he went, leaving me. Soon, Elsa was a second wife for my father. She gave birth to a boy named Moses, who, today, lives with his family where the trail starts for Puerto Loma. Soon after Moses was born, my mother gave birth to my sister Margarita. Elsa started to fight with Emilia. She wanted to take my mother's place as the "most important" wife. She wanted to order Emilia around, but it was Emilia who took care of my father, cooking for him and washing his clothes. Emilia grew so distraught that she ran away, but my uncle found her and brought her back. My father told Elsa that she could stay as a second wife, but that Emilia would always be the first wife and give the orders. Then Emilia had a baby boy they named Alberto, and Elsa had a girl. Elsa had a habit of running away, but my father always went to find her and bring her home again.

One of my earliest memories took place when my mother was pregnant with my brother, Alberto. We were all traveling on the river in a very heavily loaded canoe. The canoe started to sink. My father dived overboard to lighten the canoe, but it sank anyway. My mother grabbed me in one arm and Margarita in the other and tried to swim to the shore using only her feet. Her head disappeared under the water. In all the chaos, someone saw the dire situation and called to my father, "Luis, Emilia is drowning!" He jumped into the water and grabbed the two of us girls. With her hands freed, and her daughters safe, my pregnant mother swam to shore.

My father made a big *maloca* (big roof under which several families could live). Five families could live in this house so that he could have workers. He also made a little house quite a long distance away, where our family lived. No one else lived in that area in those days, only our family. For people believed this place to be dominated by evil spirits and were afraid. They thought that land to be under a curse. If anyone went there, they grew sick, and many died. Others died a violent death; but my father wasn't afraid. He believed in a Creator of the world.

The girl Elsa gave birth to didn't learn to walk. She was left in the small house while everyone else went to eat in the maloca. One day Father asked God about Elsa's sick little girl. Although she was almost five years old, she had never walked. As he sought an answer to the problem, he had a vision. In it, he saw a city, and he heard a woman's voice asking him what he wanted. He said, "I am looking for my daughter who is lost." In this vision, Elsa's child was on the other side of a fence. A voice spoke to him and said, "You and the child's mother didn't want her and left her alone. I heard her cry, went and found her, and took her away. I'm not giving her back. You can see her, but you can't touch her." The next day, the child died. My father was very sad.

Our family continued to grow. My mother, Emilia, had my brother Luis. Then Elsa had a boy, who died when he was fifteen. Elsa also had Benjamin and Sandra, who are still alive, but two of her daughters died – Carolina when she was thirty-five, and Paola, who was only fourteen. After Luis was born, my mother had five more children: Patricia, Berta, Maria, Juan Féliz, and Marta.

We all worked hard, but nothing went very well. In 1974, my father decided we must move back to the land of his father. That was Puerto Loma. We all left the land our father had homesteaded in Puerto Cerro from 1950 to 1974, and we went to Puerto Loma. There, we had to start all over again.

## Chapter Seven

# The Rubber Trade

Over 150 years ago, the sap of the rubber tree was discovered to be a valuable product in the world economy. In the country of Brazil, just over the border from where my people live to this day, Indian people were enslaved both economically and physically to produce rubber. Since the rubber trees needed to grow in a jungle setting surrounded by all kinds of other jungle trees, it couldn't be cultivated in a plantation. Rubber producers decided to use the local Indians to tap the rubber trees scattered throughout the jungle. The extruded sap was made into sheets of latex, which were shipped down the rivers to civilization. This trade made a lot of money for many people, but not for the Indians. The first of the men to profit from this commodity were former slave traders with no compassion for the Indian people. They didn't even see the Indians as human. The Indians were treated even worse than the black people under slavery in the United States.

If the Indians did not produce enough of the raw rubber, terrible punishments were inflicted. Limbs were cut off; eyes were blinded or sewn shut; some were burned to death; many women and girls were raped. If they tried to run away, they were caught and killed. They were pressed to pay high prices for food, cheap cloth, and other commodities, which forced them to keep searching the jungles for rubber in order to pay their ever-growing debts. Later, when I came to Florida, I learned that some 40,000 Indians died from disease and atrocities in Brazil during the years of the rubber business. Entire tribes and cultures were wiped out.

Although much of this inhumane treatment of Indians in Brazil had come to an end by my father's time, the rubber trade had crossed over the border into our part of Colombia. All the Indians of the small tribes in our area were contracted to spread out through the jungle and tap the rubber trees (similar to the way maple trees are tapped in Vermont for their sap to make maple syrup).

While no documented record exists of any physical atrocities like the ones which happened in Brazil, the Vaupés Indians were brought into economic bondage. They were dependent on the rubber trader, a non-Indian from the Brazilian or Colombian cultures, for their food supply, cloth to make dresses and pants, cooking utensils, machetes, flashlights, and other things. These items were brought into the jungle and sold on credit to the Indians, who spent their entire waking hours going through the jungle in search of rubber. Traders jacked up the prices for these staple supplies, and the Indians racked up debt they could never expect to pay off in their lifetime.

My father was the rubber boss in the area he carved out in the region of Caño Ti and Puerto Cerro. He overcame many obstacles, including trying to raise rubber in a plantation setting (which didn't work). After much hard work and perseverance, he was finally doing quite well.

You might think the Indians would be happy to have an Indian boss, but the very fact he was an Indian turned them against him. Several of the Indians who worked under him became envious. In their hearts, they questioned why he, another Indian, should be over them. They were jealous. He had two wives, and more possessions than they did. They wanted to knock him down and take his place.

Our family lived at our farm near Sircacia. One night, while my father slept, some of these jealous Indians snuck in and forced poison down his throat. With his life in danger, he started at once for the big maloca to try to save his life. An old man told him of a medicinal plant that would work as an antidote. Fortunately, my father found the plant quickly. They brewed a tea made from the leaves of this plant. Father drank it and felt better right away, but not completely well. For months, he continued to drink this tea until he was restored to full health.

After spending three months at the big maloca, we went back to our farm in Sircacia. Almost a year later, my father's enemies learned he was alive and working on his farm. They came back to finish the job. My mother and Elsa, with most of the children, had gone off to get food from one of our gardens. I stayed behind to care for my two little brothers, Luis, who was a baby, and Alberto, who was about three. I was about eight years old at this time.

My father came back from a hard day's work and was resting in his hammock. After a short time, voices echoed from the river. Men were coming in a canoe and making a lot of noise. Others came on foot, about seven in all. Before my father knew what was happening, they surrounded him, carrying guns, machetes, and clubs. They had come to kill my father.

They grabbed my father's loaded gun from a rack high up on the wall and hit it on the ground, trying to make it go off. All this time, I watched unseen, not knowing what to do. The men swore, jumped up and down, and hit and pushed my father over and over again. My father signaled to me to take the boys and run away. Luis was about one and a half years old, but he was heavy. I put him on my back and ran into the jungle with Alberto. I stumbled and fell on the jungle floor. I huddled, watching, trying to keep my brothers quiet.

The men kept hitting my father and hurting him. He was bleeding all over. One man raised a rock and hit my father in the head, intending to kill him. My father saw the rock coming and moved his head to one side. The rock hit him a glancing blow in the eye. So much blood! His body was covered in blood. His attackers stood around him, sure he was dead.

Just then, my father's friend and foreman, Juanico, came running and shouting to defend my father. "Stop! Stop! Don't kill him!" he yelled. My father lost consciousness. The men thought they had killed him, and with the job done, they ran away.

From my place in the jungle, I listened. When I heard no more noise, I brought the children back. I was so scared and sad to see my father like that. I wanted to clean him up.

"No, don't touch me," he said. "I'll be all right." He tried to clean himself up a little with a big towel, but fresh blood still oozed from his injuries. "Stay here and wait for your mother to come back. Juanico will take me to the big maloca. From there, I'll have someone take me to Mitú."

It so happened, that on his way, he met my mother and Elsa on their way back to the farm. They were very upset to see my father injured like that. He told them he was going for help and that they should go back to the farm where I was waiting.

My mother and I and the others left at the farm were frightened the bad men would come back. We hid out in the jungle and survived on food gathered from the jungle and under the cover of darkness from our gardens at night. We didn't dare start a fire to cook anything.

At night we stayed in two little canoes, floating on the caño. The little children slept, but the rest of us were awake all night. Out on the water we had other things to fear, like anacondas, alligators, and snakes – as well as the bad men. We had no blankets, no mosquito nets. I was the oldest of all the children and tried to help my mother keep everyone quiet. We were so scared!

When my father arrived in Mitú, he found a miracle had happened. The day before he arrived, an eye specialist had come to that tiny little hospital out in the middle of the jungle. Water and a black liquid leaked from his injured eye. The specialist explained that in another half hour he would have lost the sight in that eye. They took him right into surgery. He stayed in Mitú for about three weeks, and then he came home. The doctor told him that in six months he needed to go to Villavicencio for another surgery. He did this, and his sight was saved.

Although my father treated the Indians who worked under him honestly, they hated him, because he had more money than they did. They wanted to get rid of him and be the bosses. My father did not want to risk his own safety or that of his family any longer, so he decided to move to Puerto Loma, the traditional lands of his family. There were no rubber trees in that part of the jungle, but my father planned to plant trees there. We were forced to live mostly on yuca, plantains and other things that could be grown in the jungle, and fish from the river.

It took six years before my father could pay off his debts and become free to move to Puerto Loma. Our family stayed near the big maloca in our own little house. During this time, this area became a community named Puerto Cerro. My father and Juanico made trips back to the farm at Sircacia to work and earn money to pay off the debts. Finally, in 1974, we were able to move. The people who had worked for my father came into the area, and now Sircacia is a small city, big enough to be on the maps of Colombia. My father was the founder of Sircacia, and also of Puerto Cerro.

## Chapter Eight

## Puerto Loma to Bonita Springs

After his debts were paid, my father took Margarita and Alberto, together with Elsa and her children, and traveled to Puerto Loma. Only my father knew where it was. No one had lived there for a long time, but my father identified the spot by remembering the trees. He found the place where the old maloca had been. They stayed temporarily at the Yurutí village of Consuelo, about an hour away, where we had relatives.

They cleared land, built a house, and planted fruit trees, yuca, and other crops. About six months later, he came back to Puerto Cerro. He brought Margarita with him, and the others stayed at Consuelo. Father came to get us to take us to Puerto Loma. Before we could leave, he had to build canoes. He built three, each one could carry ten people, but we needed that much space to carry our belongings. It took about a year for us to get ready to move.

We had to leave our little house, our gardens, and everything familiar to us. In preparation, we made rations of fariña and packed lots of seeds. We also carried all of my father's implements for the rubber business, and even took three kinds of live fish to plant in the water of Caño Paca. The rubber trees my father planted at Puerto Loma didn't grow well. Soil in that part of the jungle was too sandy. They grew to a certain height, started turning brown, and died.

When we first arrived at Puerto Loma, we lived by the river. Every few years, the thatched roof on our home leaked. Each time, we built another house a little further from the river. The land was hilly and soon we lived up on a hill. That is why the village is called Puerto Loma (hill).

One year during the dry season, our house caught fire and burned down with everything in it. That included the tools for the rubber business. As far as our family was concerned, that was a very sad day, for it basically ended my father's dreams for a prosperous future.

When we were quite small and Margarita was about six, my mother made her a dress with a waist sewed onto a skirt. Margarita climbed a tree to pick some fruit, but lost her footing and fell to the ground. Her skirt caught on the branch of the tree and tore free of the waist. Margarita landed on the ground wearing only the bodice of the dress, while the skirt dangled in the tree. After that, we wore *batas*, one-piece dresses made like nightgowns, until I was about fifteen and learned to make what I called "real dresses" with waists and sleeves. These dresses and skirts were very long, and I made them for my mother and sisters. All of the sewing was done by hand with some help from Margarita.

At first, our father didn't want us to go to school. He wanted us to be raised like him and his father before him, without any education, but later he changed his mind. After we moved to Puerto Loma, my father said that Margarita and I could go to school if we wanted to. We attended school a little bit in Puerto Cerro, but we didn't learn anything. The teachers there only had a fifth grade education, and didn't really know how to teach. Plus, they taught in Spanish, and we didn't know any Spanish.

After moving to Puerto Loma, the first place we went to school was Consuelo. We walked for half an hour and took a little canoe for another half an hour. After several years, we finished the school at Consuelo, but we wanted to continue studying, so we found another school at San Luis de Paca. This school was further away. We walked for one hour; then it took two hours in the little canoe to get upstream to San Luis. Coming home we were going downstream, so it only took one hour in the canoe and then another hour on the trail. We left home each day at five a.m. and arrived home at seven p.m.

The next year, we found a place to stay in San Luis de Paca. This avoided so much traveling, but as my family didn't have any money, we found it hard to get enough food to eat in San Luis. Also, we had no money to buy cloth to make dresses, and we each had just two dresses to wear.

After we finished going to school, my Aunt Cecilia visited. She was a Yurutí, but from a different village. When she was young, she married a man from the Spanish-speaking culture who worked in the rubber trade. Aunt Cecilia wanted to help us, and recognized Margarita was a bright girl with an out-going personality. She offered to take Margarita with her out of the jungle to work in the home of a family in Bogotá, the capital of Colombia, and to make some money. She told Margarita to get ready. Later, she would return to get her and take her to San Martin, a medium-sized town in the department (state) of Meta, and then send her on to the family in Bogotá.

My mother's youngest boy, Juan Féliz, was about three years old at this time. Somehow when he was a baby, my mother's milk dried up. She did her best to raise him by feeding him yuca water and other food she could find, but he didn't grow properly. At three, he still couldn't walk. There was no money to take him to the doctor in Mitú or to buy him milk or vitamins. I thought it would be wonderful to earn some money to help Juan Féliz, so Margarita said, "You should be the one to go."

I shook my head. "No, she invited you."

Margarita packed a suitcase, but it wasn't for her, it was for me. When Aunt Cecilia returned, she asked, "Is the niece ready to go?"

Margarita jumped right up. "Yes, she is all ready, and here is her suitcase." And off I went with my Aunt Cecilia.

When we reached San Martin, we learned that the family in Bogotá who wanted a girl to work for them had already found a girl, so I didn't have a job. My Aunt Cecila had many daughters, and I became just one more in the house. Soon after our arrival, we all went to live in Mapiripán, a large town out in the *llanos* (the plains area of Colombia). Neftalí, Aunt Cecilia's husband, was mayor of that town for a while. One of their daughters married a North American named Russell Stendal, who owned a small airplane. Her name was Marina.

One day Marina came from San Martin to visit. She said to her mother, "You have too many girls here in this house. Let me have Filomena to help me." Aunt Cecilia agreed, so I went to help Marina. Russell came to pick me up in the little airplane. That was my first airplane ride.

Russell and Marina had a baby girl named Lisa. We lived in a big house in San Martin when Russell's parents, Chad and Patricia, came back from the United States. One week later, communist guerrillas kidnapped Russell. Lisa was just nine-months old. We were all very sad and worried about Russell. One of Russell's best friends, a Colombian man named Guillermo Romero, had not gone with Russell in the airplane the day he was kidnapped. Afterward, he came to San Martin. During the time Russell was held in captivity, Guillermo and I became good friends, and he asked me to marry him.

When I told Marina and the others that I wanted to marry Guillermo, the news shocked everyone. Aunt Cecilia took me to her house to live with her, and she counseled me in our Yurutí language to see if I really wanted to marry a Spanish-speaking man outside of our tribe. She had done the same thing herself many years ago, and it had worked out well. Her husband, Neftalí, also talked with Guillermo, and told him the good and bad things about marrying a Yurutí girl. We decided to go ahead with our plans. Culturally mixed marriages were not a new thing in the family. Marina also had a mixed marriage by marrying Russell, a "gringo", as North Americans were called in Colombia.

After five months, the guerrillas released Russell from captivity. (You can read his story in two books, *Rescue the Captors* by Russell Stendal and *The Guerrillas Have Taken Our Son* by Chad and Pat Stendal.) When he arrived in San Martin, he was very surprised to find Guillermo and me living together. He warned Guillermo that the guerrillas also had him on their list of people to be killed. We all went to the United States Embassy in Bogotá. The American officials were so happy Russell had been released unharmed that they wanted to do something nice for him. They granted his request to give visas to Guillermo and me so that we could travel to the United States with him and Marina. This was in February 1984.

The first place we stopped was to visit with Russell's grandparents in Bonita Springs, Florida. His grandparents were old and really couldn't live by themselves anymore. In their younger years, they enjoyed several trips on cruise ships. Guillermo once worked on cruise ships and knew the right words in English to wait on the old couple and to make them happy. They invited us to stay with them and take care of them while Marina and Russell continued their trip. They called Guillermo "Bill", and me "Gino". We stayed with them for many years, and eventually, our daughter, Ana Lucia, was born. Bill and I bought a little house in the area. He worked as a waiter in a very nice hotel.

**The three of us at the Regency Hotel in Florida**

## Chapter Nine

# My Words Impact My Father

After we moved to Florida, my husband and I became active in an evangelical church. We were baptized, and legalized our marriage in the United States. In 1989, we went back to Colombia for a visit, taking our two-year-old daughter, Ana, with us. The long trip to Puerto Loma was difficult. Ana became sick, and the primitive living was hard on all of us, but I enjoyed many good talks with my father. We showed him pictures of our baptism and our marriage, and told him how, under God, we had committed ourselves to each other for life.

All through the years, Elsa continued the habit of running away. Each time, she gave her older children to my father, and she would take the younger ones with her. When this happened, my father always chased after her and brought her back. While I was there, my father confided in me about Elsa. She had run away again. He said, "I'm old and sick. I don't feel I have the strength to go after her again." He asked my advice about what he should do.

I didn't really know what to say. I didn't feel wise enough to counsel my father. After thought and prayer, it occurred to me to suggest that maybe he should let Elsa go. Since she always ran away, maybe she didn't want to stay with him anymore. "Maybe you should let her do what she wants to do." I didn't realize the effect my words and testimony would have on him, until years later.

At that time, the only Christian presence in that part of the jungle was the Catholic Church. My brother Luis, who was about seventeen, felt a strong urge to preach God's Word to his people, but without some authority, he knew he would not be allowed to do so. He went to the Catholic Church in Mitú and asked to take a course to become a catechist, authorized to teach the catechism. (As I said earlier, later

Luis found Christ as his Savior and attended Bible school in Villavicencio.) After my visit, my father and mother also went to the Catholic Church. They took the course for first communion and were legally married, committing themselves to each other for life. This was a big step in their lives.

Elsa never came back. Her children were now grown up, and she left them all with my father. Evidently she found a new life somewhere else.

# Part III

# My Later Visits

# Chapter Ten

# My Father's Last Years

I continued to visit my family as often possible, but my trips were infrequent. By 2011, economic times in Florida grew more difficult. My job sewing draperies came to an end, but I found work as a babysitter. One of my main clients was a couple with triplets. The three little toddlers were a handful, and the parents appreciated my help very much. I saved my money to help my family in Colombia and never thought to ask anyone else for help.

To travel to the Vaupés, where my family lived, was expensive. First the flight to Bogotá, followed by another flight to Villavicencio to visit Margarita, and another flight from Villavicencio to Mitú. On top of all this, there was the cost to rent the canoe, motor, pay the man who operated the motor, and the price of the gasoline. Added to this was the cost of whatever gifts I carried to the folks at Puerto Loma. These gifts ranged from medicine to food treats, along with clothing I brought from Florida. Then of course, the whole process had to be reversed in order for me to get back to Bill and Ana in Bonita Springs.

Luis moved to Mitú so his two daughters could attend school. He still made trips to Puerto Loma to hold Christian meetings

**Luis in the chapel**

in the little chapel they had built. Aside from Puerto Loma, he also made trips to the other Yurutí villages where some of our more distant relatives lived. These Indians were quite amazed by the message Luis brought and by the meetings at Puerto Loma. At the beginning they opposed Luis, but later they warmed up to him, and some started attending the meetings in the chapel. My cousin Hector found he was blessed with a ministry to children, and the two of them served together. Whenever Luis ministered to the adults, Hector led a meeting for the children. My brother-in-law Francisco also started to take part. Several others came to minister to the Yurutí at Puerto Loma. Among these was a Christian Cubeo man. The Cubeos are a tribe closely related to the Yurutí. Actually, my mother is from this tribe.

By this time, Margarita's children were pretty well grown up. Her oldest daughter, Nelsy, was married and lived in Villavicencio. Olga, the youngest, was finishing high school. In Colombia, the boys have to go into the army for military training at age eighteen or after they finish high school. Carlos, the oldest boy, finished his service, married, and found a job with the army. Jorge, who couldn't go into the army because of asthma, worked on the farm with his father. José finished his army service and worked in construction. The other boy, Ricardo, is still in the army. In spite of Margarita's poverty and difficult living conditions, her children all survived and seem to be doing quite well.

**My mother with a grandchild, Luis, my father, and Margarita**

Telephone communication with my family became more frequent. Sometimes Margarita called me from Villavicencio, and sometimes Luis called me from Mitú. Usually the calls were to tell me one of our family members was sick. If I had some money, I sent it to Margarita or Luis to buy medicine and take it to the one who was sick, or to pay for transportation to take them to the doctor in Mitú.

**Alberto and most of his children**

In April 2007, one of Alberto's sons died. He was a boy about 10 years old. At the time, Alberto had traveled to Mitú to work, but became sick and was dying in the hospital there. Alberto's wife brought their sick son to Mitú. The boy was very sick with hepatitis. He died that night in the room right next to his father, Alberto. The irony is that no one in the family knew Alberto had fallen ill or that he was in the hospital. It was a very sad time for the family, but Alberto got well and returned to Puerto Loma.

In early 2011, my sister Patricia also lost a son of about sixteen. He was sent to San José in the territory of Guaviare, a town with more facilities than Mitú. There they operated, probably for appendicitis, and with the incision still open, they sent him to Villavicencio. After a blood transfusion, he became worse. He asked for spiritual help, and a priest was sent to him. Although he seemed better and started to eat a little solid food, he died.

**Patricia Stendal, Ana, Bill with Esther, me, and Nikky, Pat's granddaughter**

In September 2011, Luis called to say our old father was not doing well. I asked for two weeks off from my job and made the long trip to Puerto Loma. Upon my arrival, I found that although my mother seemed well, my father's health was failing. He responded to prayer and special care and felt better by the time I returned to Florida.

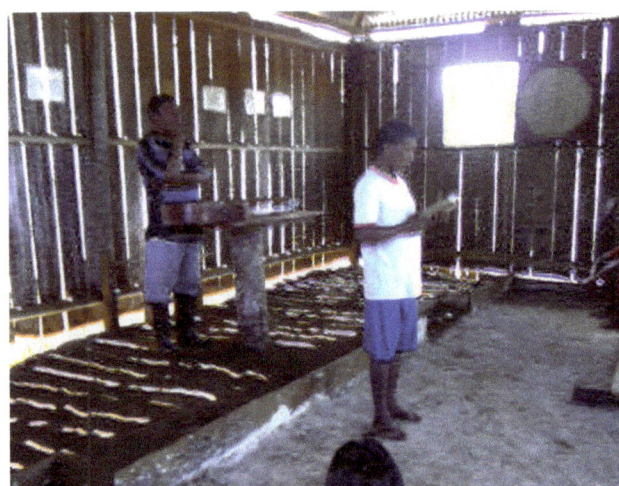

Luis behind the pulpit and Francisco reading in the chapel

Part of the congregation

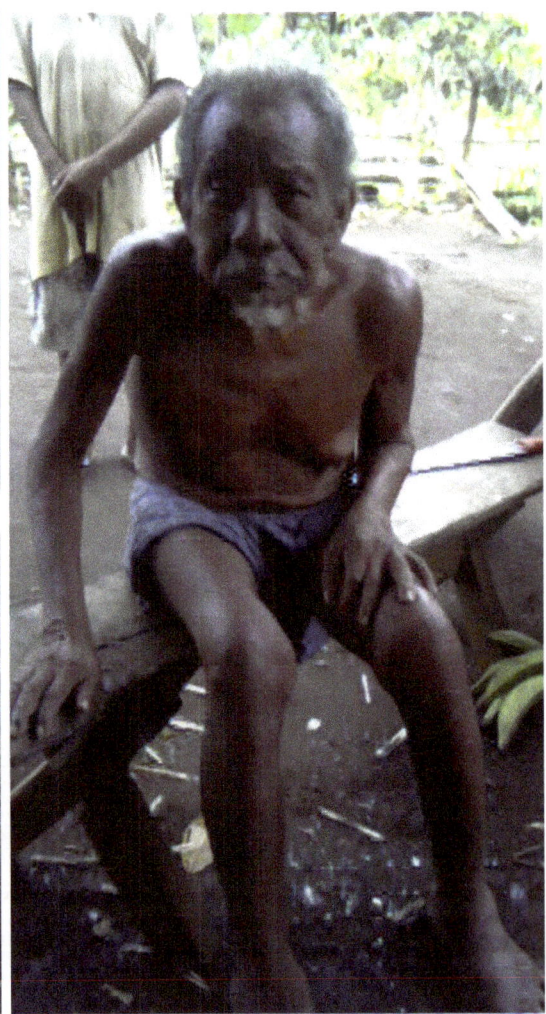

My father

In 2012, more problems arose among my family. My father became ill again, and also Carolina, one of Elsa's daughters, was very ill. Carolina, who was thirty-five years old, was taken to San José, where she underwent gall bladder surgery. It must not have gone well because she was moved to Villavicencio, and then on to Bogotá. Luis called Margarita, and she scraped together a little money; and with the help of a kind taxi driver almost miraculously found Carolina in a hospital in the huge city of Bogotá.

After Margarita sat by Carolina's side in the hospital for several days and nights, a hospital employee befriended her and let her bathe and sleep in her nearby apartment. She even lent clothes to Margarita so that she could wash and dry her own. Margarita called me from Bogotá to tell me about our father and Carolina.

I didn't have any work at that time (the triplets had started school), nor any money, but I felt in my heart that I needed to go. I prayed and told my pastor about the problem in Colombia. The pastor's wife showed great concern. "You don't have any money, or any work," she said, "but you have to go." The church took up a special collection, and it was enough to buy all my tickets.

I traveled to Colombia as quickly as I could arrange for my trip. I learned Carolina had been moved to Villavicencio again. Unfortunately, she passed away before I arrived, but Margarita told me she died trusting the Lord.

**Me with airplane**

**Airport in Villavicencio**

I made the long trip out to Puerto Loma and found my father, Luis Sr., in his hammock with swollen, infected feet. My sister Marta cared for him the best she could in the primitive situation, but he was very sick. He burned with fever and experienced a lot of pain. I brought him vitamins, pain pills, antibiotics, and antibiotic cream. During the two weeks I stayed there, I made him good nutritious soup every day, and treated him with the medicine I had carried with me. I prayed continually day and night. I wanted him to have a peaceful death, without so much pain and agony.

After about ten days, he got up and started to walk, but his legs were stiff and weak. His body had become very, very thin. He was weak and dizzy, and he fell often. It was hard to take care of him because he wanted to get up and walk. We did our best to convince him to stay in his hammock so he wouldn't fall anymore. My father felt better, so I left him in the care of my sister Marta, and my mother. I went to Villavicencio and stayed a few days with Margarita.

When I returned to Florida, Luis called me and told me the family had decided Margarita needed to go to Puerto

**The end of my visit**

**Margarita in her kitchen**

**Me with Nelsy, Olga, Margarita, and a nephew from Puerto Loma**

**Margarita washing clothes**

Loma. Since Margarita didn't have any money, and neither did they, they looked to me for help with her transportation. This news distressed me. I had no work and no money, and the church had taken up a collection once, so I couldn't ask them again. I was so upset. With much effort, I scraped together a little money and managed to buy a ticket for Margarita from Villavicencio to Mitú. Alberto met her in Mitú, and they went to Puerto Loma. My father had been calling for me and especially for my brother Alberto, his oldest son. Luis stayed in Mitú waiting for me.

According to Yurutí custom, my elderly father felt he needed to impart his spirit to his heir. I was the oldest in the family, Margarita was second, and Alberto was next. Alberto was his male heir.

Several years before, Alberto had been asked to receive the spirit of a dying uncle. The spirit involved caused Alberto a lot of trouble and suffering. It caused him to drink and fight, and this led to trouble for his wife. Alberto had received the message of the gospel but was not mature in his faith. He did not have the spiritual fortitude to easily resist the effect of this spirit. He ran away from Puerto Loma, and it took him years to get free from the bad effects. Because of this, he didn't want to receive any more spirits from dying relatives, even from his own father, and for this reason, he avoided coming to Puerto Loma. Luis was the next son in line, but he was deemed to be too civilized to receive this impartation.

My father also called for me as his oldest child, but I was still in Florida trying to figure out where I could find the money to finance another trip. Margarita arrived and saw he received a little better care, but our father agonized for Alberto. Finally, Alberto arrived and received the impartation from Father. Happily, it didn't cause him any ill effects.

My father, who had been raised in the town of Mitú by non-Indian foster parents, had come under the teaching of the Catholic Church. Although he returned to the Indian way of life as a young adult, he maintained a strong belief in a Creator-God, and he cultivated a relationship with Him. Soon after my first visit back to my homeland, my father and mother went to Mitú and established their relationship with the church. He believed in salvation through Jesus Christ. Later, under the teaching of Luis and from my visits, he became stronger in his faith. He had no evil spirit to impart to Alberto.

One time Bill's sister Martha, who used to help me at times, told me that if anything happened to my father and I needed to go to Puerto Loma, she would help me. In my heart, I felt I needed to go to my father, so I decided to call my sister-in-law Martha. She was in Spain, but she answered her cell phone. She understood my desire and arranged through her daughter in Florida to buy the tickets I needed. As soon as I could, I flew to Bogotá, but learned I had to wait four days for a flight to Mitú because all the flights were fully booked. I called Luis and told him to go ahead without me, leaving my sister Maria in Mitú to travel to Puerto Loma with me.

My sister-in-law Lucy met me in Bogotá, and we went to her house. She quickly realized my situation. She took her Bible, and we read and prayed together. We interceded for my father, that he would be under the control of the Holy Spirit and have the peace of God. We also prayed he wouldn't be frightened. Four hours passed before we realized it.

We went to bed. In the middle of the night, a gust of wind awakened me. It came in through the door of my room, passed around my bed, and went out through the other window. It was a gentle wind, but it woke me up. I sat up in the bed, and I thought, *It's gone.* When I arrived in Mitú, my nephew Carlos was there to receive me. He brought me the news that my father had died.

Before he died, my father had not received food or beverages for a while, and was in a semi-conscious condition. One day he awakened. Margarita made him a special meal, which he ate with her help. Together with Alberto, she took him out of his hammock and cleaned him all up, then helped him back into his hammock. He went into a deep sleep and peacefully passed away. I was surprised and saddened, but his death was not unexpected. I continued on to Puerto Loma to be with my grieving family, especially my mother. Amid my personal sorrow, I was happy my beloved father had died peacefully, surrounded by a loving family and trusting in Jesus Christ as his Savior.

Me with Margarita in 2012

With my husband Bill in Florida

## Chapter Eleven

# First Anniversary of My Father's Death

Since my visits to Puerto Loma in 2012, and the deaths of my father and my half-sister Carolina, I had been very concerned about my family. On one of those visits, I met my niece Aleida, one of Alberto's daughters. I took a picture of her with her husband and baby. Her husband was a good-looking young man, but he seemed to have a problem. He had bought a tee shirt from a peddler on the river and seemed to be unusually attached to this shirt. It was more than a normal fondness for a favorite shirt. He could hardly take it off long enough to be washed and dried. If he wasn't wearing that shirt, he said he didn't feel good.

I kept in close touch with Luis and Margarita by telephone, and I was terribly shocked to learn Aleida's husband had taken his own life. He hanged himself. I looked at the picture I had taken, and to my surprise, I realized the black tee shirt he was so attached to had Satanic or demonic pictures on the front. I hadn't noticed that before. Although I had helped as a checker

**Aleida with her husband and child**

for the American couple who were translating the New Testament in Yurutí, I hadn't heard recently of any progress being made. I grieved for my people in the Vaupés. How much they needed to have the New Testament in their own language and grow in the Lord.

I continued to gather clothing and save money, and in 2013, I made another trip to the Vaupés to be with my family for the first anniversary of my father's death. I found my mother in Mitú at Luis' house. She seemed to be in good health. Many of my relatives were in Mitú right then. School vacation had just started, and the adults had come to take their children back to the village. One of my nephews had won an electronic tablet in school. All of the children were very excited about this. The excitement continued as I opened my duffel bags and started distributing the clothing I had brought.

**With Margarita, Luis, my mother and others in Mitu**

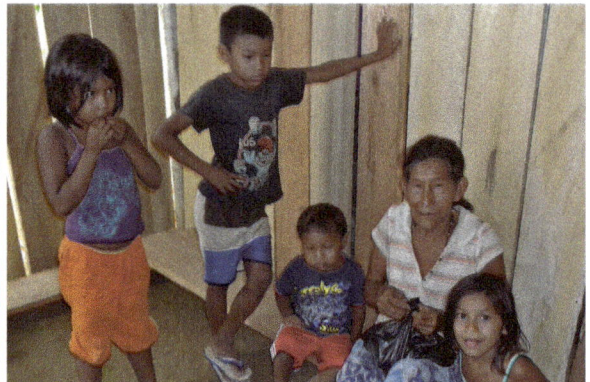
**My mother with some of her grandchildren**

**I distribute some of the clothing I brought from Florida**

**With some of my family in Mitu**

The trip to Puerto Loma was challenging, as usual. First, we traveled down the big Vaupés River, and once we turned into Caño Yi, we faced the many rapids. To lighten the canoe many of us were forced to walk, leaving the most experienced to guide the canoe up through the rapids. Juan Féliz and the baby had to stay in the canoe. Once we navigated past the rapids, we took a break. My sisters found food for a snack. After we rested and ate, we continued up the Caño Yi, but travel proved to be slow. Many fallen trees blocked our way. Sometimes it took as long as half an hour to clear away logs and branches so the canoes could pass.

**Organizing the canoes to go to Puerto Loma**

**Some of my relatives with Juan Feliz in the yellow**

**Luis running the motor, the mother in the tan cap, and Margarita with some granddaughters**

**My brother-in-law Francisco standing and my mother in the foreground**

# FIRST ANNIVERSARY OF MY FATHER'S DEATH

The baby isn't sure he likes to be left with Juan Feliz

Luis and Francisco slowly move the canoe up the rapids

Safely on the other side, we stop for a rest

My sisters look for food for a snack

Someone takes my picture

Enjoying a break

Luis guides the canoe under another obstacle

We also got through this one

Upper Cano Yi is calmer but many trees have fallen

My sisters look very tired

Finally we arrive at the portage

Finally, we came to the place where we disembarked. We left the canoes and took a trail through the jungle to another caño. By this time, the sky peeking through the jungle canopy was getting dark. We hung our hammocks under a roof we erected for that purpose, a Yurutí hotel.

In the morning, we organized backpacks to carry all our belongings and supplies over the portage trail. This usually takes two hours, but we found the trail more difficult than usual.

**A roof gives us a place to hang our hammocks**

**The next morning we repack to head down the trail**

**Each one carries a load**

**Even my mother has a big load**

**Marta has to help her little boy**

**The trail becomes very wet**

Part of the trail disappeared under water. At the end of the trail, we boarded other canoes for the rest of the trip to Caño Paca and Puerto Loma. It was so good to be back again.

Buildings in the tropics do not last long, especially when they are made of wood. It was time to replace the chapel in Puerto Loma. Luis and some of the others were working on this project. I found my mother in rather good health for her age. Her youngest son, Juan Féliz, was close to her. This was

**It is good that Mother has rubber boots**

**Some stop for a rest**

**We are all getting tired**

**We are happy to arrive at Puerto Loma**

the little brother for whom I left my home in the first place, because I wanted to send money to take him to the doctor in Mitú and to buy him milk and vitamins. I was able to send some money, but since we left Colombia and went to Florida, it wasn't so much.

My mother had lost her breast milk when he was a baby. She fed him the best she could with things like yuca water. Although he didn't die, his development was not normal. He learned to walk, but he remained vulnerable, even as an adult. Later, with my mother's last child, Marta, this problem didn't occur.

Times were difficult for the Yurutí. Opportunities to earn money were few. Outsiders were eying the Yurutí land, planning to harvest minerals they thought might be below the surface. In Colombia, all mineral rights belong to the government, not to the owners of the land. The developers would make a lot of money and introduce the evils of civilization into the Yurutí jungle.

Pray for my people. Adults, young people, and children are taking their own lives. This is a demonic happening. My people are very poor and have little means of making a living. Sometimes they are taken away by the guerrillas, the subversives. This has happened to many of the young tribal people. In this manner, the enemy has attacked my people. One time they took my nephew Carlos, but by the grace and mercy of God, my brother Alberto went and retrieved him. That was a miracle.

Luis is very happy in the construction of the new chapel, but he is suffering from pain in his knees. The pain makes it hard for him to walk or carry things, and even to sit in a canoe, which he has to do all the time. On the trail, the pain forces him to sit down and rest often. My sister Patricia has a problem in her stomach. My mother suffers from arthritis in both of her knees. Patricia, Luis' wife, also has pain in her knees. Juan Féliz has epileptic attacks. I appreciate your prayers for all of my family. Pray especially for the people of Puerto Loma, and for Luis and his companions as they bring the Word of God to the people.

**After a trip like that, there is no place like home**

# Afterword

You might like to know how this book came to be written:

I happened to come through Bonita Springs, Florida, right after Filomena returned from the trip to visit her family in 2001. She showed me the pictures she had taken and told me the story of her trip. The next year she went again, and once more I came through Bonita Springs right at the precise time to see the pictures and hear the story. Then after the third trip in 2004, I decided that this would make a wonderful story to share with others who were interested in missions and would appreciate the unique way in which God used Filomena to bring the story of salvation to her people. I asked Filomena to tell me the story again slowly, while I took notes and then translated it into English. I did not have a scanner, but we gave the pictures to Filomena's daughter Ana, who was a high school student at the time, and she said she would scan them.

Over the next few years, whenever I happened to see Filomena during my trips between Colombia, South America and the United States, I asked her about the pictures. She always said they weren't scanned yet, and then she said they were lost. To make matters worse, she had inadvertently thrown away the negatives during one of her periodic housecleaning efforts. The set of prints she had given to her mother in the jungle had been destroyed during a bad storm. I had changed laptops, and I hadn't transferred the text to my new laptop. It seems that my idea of making a book out of Filomena's story had come to an untimely end.

Then, in mid 2013, I decided to clean out some old papers from a closet here in Colombia. Imagine my surprise to find the folder with the printouts of the first four chapters of Filomena's book. Right after that, my husband got sick, and we had to go to Bonita Springs to see his doctors. While there, one of Filomena's stepsons did a search on my laptop and found all the scanned pictures from the first trips.

(Ana had scanned them after all and sent them to my laptop before the pictures got lost.) Now, with all that material, I could go ahead with the book.

Since we were in Bonita Springs eight months while my husband was recuperating, I was able to interview Filomena many times and learn her family history as well as hear the story of her last trips to her home in the jungle and receive the pictures from those trips.

A second reason that encouraged me to write this book is that it is a wonderful pictured description of life in a small indigenous tribe in the Amazon rain forest.  I was once a fourth grade teacher in Minneapolis, and in our social studies curriculum, we taught how human beings adapted to life in different areas of the world – the arctic, the mountains, the desert, and the jungles.  This book would have been a great resource.  I know now  that because of the Christian emphasis, it would have to be used in Christian schools.  I hope that the Lord will use it where He sees fit.

Another reason that I was motivated to write Filomena's story is that this is an ongoing work.  Filomena will continue to make trips, bringing help and light to her people and resources to enable Luis and the other Christians to spread the gospel.  All proceeds from the sale of this book will go to Filomena for this purpose, and the Lord may touch the hearts of some of you to help in a more extensive way as well.  The Pan-America Mission Inc., P.O.Box 429, Newberg, OR 97132 has agreed to issue tax-deductible receipts through Colombia Para Cristo to those who wish to donate to this ministry.  Please write your check to Pan-America Mission and include a post-it or other note designating it for the Yuruti ministry or for Filomena.  As we approach the end of this age, it is heart-warming to see how the Lord is using unusual means so that every tribe and nation will be reached with His message and join us praising God around the throne.

God bless you, each one.

Patricia C. Stendal

## Meet the Author

Filomena left her home in the jungle when she was about 20 years old to earn money to help a handicapped brother. Circumstances brought her all the way to Florida where she adapted to life in America; the plight of her family called her back in 2001. Since then she has made trips to help, bringing clothing and other needed items, but best of all, she has brought the message of Jesus Christ. Filomena lives in Florida with her husband Bill. They have one daughter and three grandchildren.

# Books written by the Stendal Family

High Adventure in Colombia
    by Chad Stendal

The Guerrillas Have Taken Our Son
    by Chad & Pat Stendal

Walking In The Spirit
    by Chadwick Martin Stendal

40 Years in Colombia
Lomalinda: There and Back Again
    by Patricia & Gloria Stendal

This Gospel of the Kingdom
    by Chad Stendal

Are Millions of Christians Really Safe?
    by Chad Stendal

The Problem Christ Came to Solve
    by Chad Stendal

Rescue The Captors
    by Russell Stendal

The Beatitudes: God's Plan For Battle
    by Russell Stendal

The Tabernacle of David
    by Russell Stendal

The Elijah Who Is To Come
    by Russell Stendal

…And The Earth Shall Respond To The Wheat…
    by Russell Stendal

All proceeds from the book will go to Filomena to be used for the Yuruti tribe. Donations, not book sales, will receive tax-deductible receipts.

Donations can be made through:

In the USA:
Chad & Pat Stendal
Pan America Mission Inc., P.O. Box 429,
Newberg, Oregon, USA 97132-0429
http://www.panamericamission.org/

## TO ORDER ANY OF THE THESE BOOKS

Ordering books in the USA:
www.Amazon.com
www.AnekoPress.com
Or, Dwight A. Clough, 1223 West Main Street #228
Sun Prairie, Wisconsin 53590 USA
Phone (608) 834-8291
books@dwightclough.com
www.dwightclough.com/Stendal

## PARA PEDIR ALGUNO DE ESTOS LIBROS EN COLOMBIA

Colombia para Cristo:
Avenida Caracas No. 46-81 • Local
Telefax: 3461419 • Celular: 317-2219175
Correo: cpclibros@hotmail.com
www.fuerzadepaz.com

www.ingramcontent.com/pod-product-compliance
Lightning Source LLC
Chambersburg PA
CBHW061128070526
44584CB00033B/4254